"Most of the Western
December 25th. J.D. G
means. And his excellen

STEVE GAINES, Pastor, Bellevue Baptist Church,
Memphis, Tennessee

"J.D. unpacks the longings each of us feel around Christmastime, unearthing the questions we all ask deep down and
pointing to answers. I highly recommend this!"

GREG LAURIE, Senior Pastor, Harvest Church, California,
and Evangelist for Harvest Crusades

"It's easy to think that we understand the Christmas story.
Bethlehem, star, baby in an animal pen, wise men. Check.
Check. We've heard it all before... but so what? This little
book, full of wisdom and understanding, will tell you why
you should care. Take a moment and read it. You may be
surprised. And your life may be changed."

ELYSE M. FITZPATRICK, Author,
Worthy: Celebrating the Value of Women

"Quite simply the most moving Christmas book I have ever
read. Profound questions get posed: Is there a God? Where
do I find help? What has he done for me? What is he like?
And with each answer I found my heart was deeply touched."

RICO TICE, Author, *Capturing God*;
Founder, Christianity Explored Ministries

"J.D. Greear tells the Christmas story in an engaging, enlight-
ening, exciting fashion that will put you in the Christmas
spirit. A fantastic Christmas gift!"

JAMES MERRITT, Pastor, Crosspointe Church, Duluth,
Georgia; Past President of the Southern Baptist Convention

"In *Searching for Christmas*, J.D. takes us beyond cultural celebrations and traditions, and guides us back to the true heart of Christmas. He refocuses our hearts on the astounding love that God demonstrated by sending his Son to this earth. Put simply, if you are overwhelmed by the chaos of Christmas, this book will help you."

ADAM W. GREENWAY, President,
Southwestern Baptist Theological Seminary

"Whether you are someone who is searching for answers to the big questions of life, or a new follower of Christ, or a seasoned believer, this funny and accessible book will point you to rich truths that are older than time but as pertinent as ever."

KERI LADOUCEUR, Founder, New Ground Network;
Exponential Host and Associate

"The Christmas hymn 'O Little Town of Bethlehem' has us sing this prayer: 'be born in us today.' Truly nothing is greater at Christmastime than the reality that the same baby who was born in the manger is changing hearts and lives two thousand years later. This little book will introduce you to the real meaning of Christmas."

TREVIN WAX, Author, *Rethink Your Self* and *This Is Our Time*

"This wonderful book shows us the One that Christmas is all about, and how he is all you will ever need, now and forever."

DANIEL L. AKIN, President,
Southeastern Baptist Theological Seminary

"I love this. Here is a winsome, wise book by a great storyteller. J.D. shows us that in the heart of everyone is a longing that only Jesus can satisfy. This Christmas, read this book: you'll be glad you did."

PAUL D. TRIPP, Author, *New Morning Mercies*

J.D. GREEAR

SEARCHING

FOR

CHRISTMAS

Searching for Christmas
© J.D. Greear, 2020
Reprinted 2020

Published by
The Good Book Company

thegoodbook.com | thegoodbook.co.uk
thegoodbook.com.au | thegoodbook.co.nz | thegoodbook.co.in

ISBN: 9781784985318 | Printed in Denmark

Design by André Parker

Contents

1. Why I Own a Fluffy Neck-Warmer

The etiquette of Christmas gift buying can be quite stressful.

When I came home for Christmas the first year I was away at college, I met up with a girl I'd been dating the year before. It was December 23rd. To be honest, it wasn't very clear what our relationship status was. (This was before Facebook, so I couldn't just check on there.) I had just left my parents' house to drive over to hers when a panicky thought struck me: "Am I supposed to have a Christmas present for her?"

My mind raced. *If she hands me a present and I have nothing for her, then this relationship is definitely over. On the other hand, if it's already over and she doesn't give me a gift, I don't want to drop $75 on a girl I have no future with.*

I found a sports store on the way, and I ran in and found a fluffy Adidas neck-warmer you wore when skiing. I thought it was perfect. It really screamed, "You're special." If she didn't want it, I could always use it. Plus, it was on sale for $7. I took it next door to a more upmarket store and persuaded them to gift-wrap it really nicely for me.

I was quite proud of myself.

I got to her house and left the present in the car. She opened the door, said "Hi," and the next thing she said was "I bought you a gift." I felt so relieved. "I got you something too," I said.

She gave me her gift. It was in a beautiful gift bag, and it was a really, really high-quality jacket. It had clearly cost a lot more than $7. My gift was not going to cut it.

I was no longer feeling so proud of myself.

So I did what any teenage guy would do. Well, what any teenage guy who happens to have a sister three years younger than him would do. I told this girl that I'd actually left my gift at home, and when we got there, I left her in the front part of the house while I found my mom in the back.

"Mom," I said, in a voice of quiet desperation, "Do you have a gift that you were going to give to my sister that she doesn't know about yet—a really nice one?"

"Why?"

"Mom, I don't really have time to entertain questions at this point—do you or don't you?"

"Yes."

I went over to the Christmas tree, found the gift, took my sister's name off it, and added this girl's to it. Then I presented it to her.

"What is it?" she asked.

"It's a surprise," I answered, more truthfully than she knew.

She opened it up. It was a sweater. An expensive one. She loved it. Phew.

The relationship, as it turned out, didn't work out (I know. You're just as shocked as I am!) To this day, as far as I know, that girl doesn't know what happened (unless she's reading this book now—in which case, I'm sorry). And to this day, though I hardly ever use it, I still own a fluffy Adidas neck-warmer.

WHAT KIND OF GIFT?

All children know that presents are at the heart of Christmas. Most of us can remember, as kids, waking up at the crack of dawn on Christmas Day and asking, "Can we get up now?" Until I was 10 or 11, that day was the best day of my year. Why? Materialism. I knew I would get lots of great gifts from people who loved me. Later, I would learn that it was fun to give good gifts to people I loved, too.

Christians believe that at the heart of Christmas, and of life, is one particular present—God's gift to us of a baby. But what kind of present is it?

Is it a gift like the one I got into the car with on that December 23rd all those years ago—non-existent? Is this baby just like the Santa Claus myth, which makes you feel comforted and sentimental in the Christmas season, but that's it, because it's just make-believe?

Or is this gift like the $7 neck-warmer—one that is given without much effort, that costs little to the giver, and that changes nothing very much?

Or is it like that jacket—carefully planned, expensively bought, and given with love?

I want to show you why God's gift to you falls into the third category. To do so, I want to rewind back through history, but not to the first Christmas and the events we're so familiar with—the manger scene, shepherds watching sheep, angels singing their songs, and wise men arriving. I want to go back further than that because there's more to the Christmas story than those oh-so-familiar events. I want to land back around 800 BC.

It was at that point that a man named Isaiah, claiming to speak as a messenger from God, announced that "the LORD himself will give you a sign: See, the virgin will conceive [and] have a son" (from the Old Testament Bible book of Isaiah, chapter 7, verse 14).

A baby was coming who would be born in the most unlikely—humanly speaking, impossible—circumstances. Now, maybe the part of the Christmas story when a virgin gets pregnant is the part where you check out and file it as myth. But I think that's the part where you should sit up and listen: because that event was foretold over 700 years before. God had been preparing for the first Christmas centuries before Mary first laid her newborn baby in a feeding trough.

This isn't a Santa Claus myth but real history (more on this in chapter 3). The most unlikely birth in human history was a "sign" from God that he is real, and that he really gets involved, because he really cares.

The people to whom Isaiah made this prophecy—the people of Israel—were desperate to hear something, anything, from God. They were, said Isaiah, a "people walking in darkness." It was a time of national crisis. Economically, they had been devastated. They were facing invasion, and so their very existence as a nation was under threat. There was a darkness of uncertainty about their future, of fear about their safety, of the feeling that they were all alone, of the sense that they were helpless and they were hopeless. There was the darkness of knowing that things had gone wrong and knowing that there was no way to put things back together the way that they were supposed to be. They were searching for something to hold on to. And God said that what they needed was the birth of a baby. What they were searching for was what he would do at the first Christmas.

As we come to the end of this year, we too know how it feels for everything we thought was certain to become suddenly uncertain. We know the sensation of the ground shifting and even sinking beneath us. We've experienced the sense that there is no way to put things back together the way they used to be. We're aware more than ever, and perhaps for the first time, that prosperity, state-of-the-art medical systems, our nation's economy, and even our own lives are more fragile than we'd like them to be.

Most of us know something of the darkness and the shadows this Christmas. Maybe this Christmas you're unsure about what the next year holds for you: your job security is shaky; your marriage is crumbling; your health is fading. Maybe this is the first Christmas that you've felt alone. Or maybe you've felt like that for longer than you can remember. Maybe you don't know where to go or where to turn. Or maybe things are ok, but still you wonder if there is more, and you sense that maybe that "more" might involve God.

We are searching for something to hold on to. And God says to us the same as he said to those people facing darkness all those centuries ago—that, perhaps without knowing it, we're searching for Christmas. Strange as it may sound, God says to us that, in times of plenty and in times of crisis, what we most need is the birth of a baby:

> "A child will be born for us,
> a son will be given to us,
> and the government will be on his shoulders.
> He will be named
> Wonderful Counselor, Mighty God,
> Eternal Father, Prince of Peace." (Isaiah 9 v 6)

FOUR NAMES

There are a lot of rules about choosing names for your children that nobody ever tells you about. For example, if you or your spouse ever dated anyone with a certain name, that name is off-limits. If a name reminds your spouse of a girl she didn't like in school, that's also off-limits. And then you need to think through how the first and last names work together. I found a list by a pastor and author, Craig Groeschel, of unfortunate name combinations of actual people (say these out loud to get the full comedic effect):[1]

Anita Mann.

Lois Price.

And my favorite: a lady named Helen who married a guy with the last name Back:

Helen Back.

Apparently after ten years of marriage, she said it was mostly true.

Names matter. That's why all of the virgin's baby's names were chosen by God. He wanted the baby's names to describe why this was the greatest gift he could give: the most valuable present ever given. In this short book, I want to take you through the four names, or titles, that Isaiah announced that this baby—the baby we usually call Jesus—would have: Wonderful Counselor. Mighty God. Eternal Father. Prince of Peace.

As we look at each, we'll see why the birth of this child is such radically good, life-changing news for us. We'll see Jesus doing things that can give us confidence that this isn't sentimental myth but historical reality, and that there's much more to the story of Christmas than we may ever have realized. We'll see that the person at the heart of Christmas gives a hope that we can hold on to when we feel helpless or hopeless.

We'll see that Jesus is a lot more valuable—and useful—than a $7 neck-warmer, or an expensive jacket, or anything else.

2. He Gets It

"Wonderful Counselor"

One of the things that we tend to miss in the Christmas story is how poor Jesus and his parents were.

Jesus was born into the worst kind of poverty. He was born a Jew, and in that period the Jews as a people were very poor and oppressed. But even for Jews, Jesus' family had fewer means than most.

Consider, for instance, the common Christmas fact that Jesus was born in an animal shelter. This was no more common in the first century than it is in the twenty-first. To begin to grasp what was going on at the first Christmas, we need to get past our cute, quaint little manger scenes with well-behaved animals. There was nothing sentimental about that first night. No woman wants to give birth to her first baby (or second, or third) amid the smell of cows, with possibly only her husband to help. People didn't have babies in barns back then for the same reason they don't today: barns are dirty, they are smelly, and they don't come with midwives.

Some people make their manger scenes smell nice by sprinkling cinnamon or nutmeg on it. But if you want your manger scene to be authentic, take some animal dung and rub it around it.

That's gross, but that's where Jesus was born. That's how poor his family was.

Jesus would also spend the whole of the rest of his life poor. For three years he was effectively homeless; he himself said that he had "no place to lay his head" (Luke 9 v 58). And, as those in poverty often are, he was sneered at by the educated and the wealthy. When he died, he had no friends, no possessions, and no reputation. His birth had set the pattern for the rest of his life.

In other words, Jesus was a PR agency's nightmare because he was in so many ways unimpressive. But for those of us who find life hard in one way or another, it's his very weakness that is life-changing. Here's why.

HE GETS IT

One of the earliest Christians, the writer of a book in the New Testament called Hebrews, described Jesus this way:

> "[He is not] unable to sympathize with our
> weaknesses ... [he] has been tempted in every
> way as we are, yet without sin. Therefore, let us
> approach the throne of grace with boldness, so that
> we may receive mercy and find grace to help us in
> time of need." (Hebrews 4 v 15-16)

This writer believed that Jesus sat (and sits) on a heavenly throne: that he is God himself, the King who rules over us (more on that in the next chapter). What's remarkable is that this is no distant God, sitting up in heaven and peering down on the mess in this world and shaking his head in sadness or "tsking" at us with annoyance. This is a God who became human, who was born in poverty and who knew what it was to be tempted, rejected, lonely, hungry, and worried. In other words, a God who knows what it's like to be us.

Jesus walked through the kinds of things that we walk through in this world. He faced many of the worst things that this world can throw at a person, which means that he can be a reliable guide to us in even the worst kinds of pain and the worst kinds of situations.

In other words, he is uniquely qualified to be your counselor.

BETTER THAN A THERAPIST

The original Hebrew word Isaiah used, which we translate "counselor," means one who advises us, instructs us, and guides us through problems from a position of authority. It doesn't just mean "therapist"; it means someone who has the experience to understand the situation, the wisdom to work out the solution, and the power to enact it. The "counselor" Isaiah is talking about is not the kind of person you call up late at night and pour out your heart to and they mirror everything you say: *Wow, that sounds terrible. Yeah, I bet that hurt. Oh, I struggle with her too.* Of course, it's great to have empathetic friends like that, and it does help to share, but if that's all your counselor does, something is missing.

Isaiah wasn't saying that Jesus would be a great listener (though he was) or know exactly what questions to ask (though he did). No, he's talking about somebody to whom you can bring your worst problems and he can show you a way out.

A few years ago I was in eastern Europe visiting a friend who had moved there, and we had to cross the border into one of the former Soviet republics. These are not cozy, friendly experiences, especially for those from the United States. Apparently they don't spend a lot of time doing customer-service trainings for the border guards over there.

I was there with the only two tools I possessed—my passport and a winning smile. That was all that I had. And I was feeling more than a little nervous because there were guys with AK47s standing around. Smiling didn't seem like it rated highly on their list of hobbies. And my nationality wasn't one with which they'd had pleasant experiences.

But my friend who lives over there had crossed this border literally hundreds of times. So when he noticed how tense I was, he said, "Don't worry about it. I got it." Every time that we had to cross a border, he would tell me where to go, who to talk to, who not to talk to, when to smile, when to look down. He knew what he was doing, and he knew what I needed to be doing. He had walked that path before.

That's the kind of "counselor" Jesus offers to be for each of us. He is saying, *The path of pain? I've endured it. Loneliness? I know it. Temptation? I know it. Betrayal? Loss? Heartache? I've walked those roads. And I can reliably show you the way through them. I can guide you across the border. Don't worry. I got it.* He is the Wonderful Counselor.

The prophecy about Jesus' birth tells us this: Jesus came for people with problems. The manner of his life confirms it—because not only did he live in homeless poverty, but at the same time he performed powerful miracles. Read any of the Gospels—the historical accounts of his life—and you'll see Jesus feeding 5,000 people with a boy's lunch; you'll see him giving sight to the blind and health to the chronically sick; you'll see him raising dead people to life.

Those miracles weren't just fun tricks to wow people or prove his power. It's not like Jesus just turned to his best friend one day and said, *Hey, Peter, do you feel like flying? Is that on your bucket list? Because I can make that happen for you* and then sent Peter soaring up. No, every miracle started with a problem—hunger, exclusion, disease, even death. And each time Jesus entered into that problem, using his miraculous power to transform it.

There were only two qualifications people needed in order to know the power of this counselor working in and for them. One, they needed to know that they had problems and accept that they couldn't fix them (what you might call humility). Two, they needed to know that he could transform them, and so come to him and ask (what you might call faith).

The traditional Christmas season is a strange time. In one sense, it's a time full of joy. Families get together. Kids get so excited that they can't sleep. Gifts are opened. Everyone smiles and watches *It's a Wonderful Life*. Yet at the same time, for many of us, it's the time that we find it hardest to bury our struggles or ignore our problems or regrets.

Maybe you're all too aware that though you've put on a great Christmas with your loved ones, you're also breaking under the burden of something that you can't cope with. Maybe you don't have any loved ones near you this Christmas at all.

Jesus gets that. He didn't come for people who have it all together. He came for people with problems. He came for people whose lives were dysfunctional and messed up. He came for people who had driven their lives into a dead end. He came for those who had been mistreated, neglected, and abused. And he came for those who had gotten everything they wanted out of life and still found it didn't give them what they were looking for. He is, uniquely, the counselor: the one who has the experience to understand the situation, the wisdom to work out the solution, and the power to enact it.

THE MOST WONDERFUL THING

So, in a sense, the most "wonderful" thing here is not the counsel, but the counselor himself. Because I'm a pastor, a lot of times I meet people who are wondering if Jesus can make their lives better. They are asking, "Can Jesus help my family? Can Jesus fix my struggling marriage? Can a relationship with Jesus help focus my career? Can it help me restore balance? Can it make me happy?"

And the answer is yes, he can help you with your problems. If you're willing to listen to his counsel, to look for his transforming power, and to accept that he may say things that are different than how you've been figuring life out up to now, then he can and will help.

But the bigger point is this: when you come to know Jesus, he gives you something far greater than the answers to those problems. He gives you himself. And who he is is even better than what he does.

You may be looking for a solution. God gives you something even better: a relationship with him. Life's greatest discovery is knowing Jesus: knowing he loves you, knowing his promise to be ever-present in your life, knowing that he promises to work all things out according to a plan that is bathed in love and executed in power. This discovery doesn't take away all your problems, but it does completely change how you go through them.

So yes, the Wonderful Counselor can solve your problems. You've got guilt? He can handle that. He was called "the friend of sinners." By his death, he came to make a way back for those far from God to get back to him.

You've got regret over past mistakes? He can help you transform them. In his resurrection he promised he could make all things new.

You've got questions about eternity, about your soul? He can answer those. He told Thomas, the disciple who doubted, that he was "the way, the truth, and the life."[2]

You've got health problems? He can walk that road with you. The Bible says he's "a man of sorrows and acquainted with grief ... He has borne our griefs and carried our sorrows." He came to give us hope in suffering.

You've got problems in your marriage or your family? He can help. "Come to me," he told a group of weary listeners, "all of you who are weary and burdened, and I will give you rest."

You've got wounds from past abuses? He can heal those. The writer of Hebrews says he can save "to the uttermost" those who come to him.

He's the Wonderful Counselor. It's why he came: why he was born in an animal shelter and grew up to have nowhere to lay his head, why he knew rejection and loneliness and weakness, why he healed the sick and fed the hungry and raised the dead—so that you could know that he understands and can turn things around. Are you ready to experience the help of a Wonderful Counselor? He extends the invitation.

3. On Your Side

"Mighty God"

Christmas is the season of choice. If you want to buy a food processor, Amazon offers you 2,000 types. Or how about a drill—there are more than 40,000 options.

No, I'm not making those numbers up.[3]

Choices can be glorious, and confusing, and empowering, and overwhelming, all at the same time.

And in the West today, it looks as though it is the same with God. There is a huge array of deities to choose from, including the "no to all" option. Walk through an airport or shopping mall anywhere and you will be walking past countless people who believe in no God, plenty of people who are of the view that there are many gods, and another great multitude who believe in one God but who have very different thoughts on what that one God is like and what he (or she, or it) thinks. For some, God is kind of a distant grandfather guy, looking down benevolently and wanting us to be happy. To others, God is a harsh taskmaster, counting up your good and bad actions and weighing up whether he's going to have mercy on you in the end. To others, God is an impersonal force that wound the universe up and is now off doing other stuff while we get on with it down here. To others, God *is* the universe.

There are so many options to choose from—it's empowering and overwhelming at the same time.

How do you know? How can you choose? And what does it matter?

WHAT KIND OF GOD?

Isaiah's claim was that the baby who would be born at the first Christmas would be "Mighty God." Notice the first big statement he's making there: that there is a God. Out there, beyond what we can see and measure, there is not nothing. There is a God. But what kind of God? What was Isaiah thinking of when he used the word "God"?

Well, because Isaiah was a member of the ancient nation of Israel, when he spoke of "God," he had a very specific God in mind—the God who had been with Israel from the time when they were just a tiny family, and who had brought them to nationhood and to the land that they lived in as Isaiah passed on his message.

This God had a name. "God" isn't a name; it's more of a category. Just about everyone in the ancient world believed in a god or gods. The question wasn't "Is there a god?" but rather "Which kind of god are you talking about?"

And one of the most crucial ways of knowing God was knowing his name.

God had told his name to his people hundreds of years before Isaiah's time, to another member of Israel, Moses. Moses lived at a time when the people of Israel were slaves, oppressed by Egypt. And one day, at a burning-but-not-destroyed bush, God told Moses that he was going to rescue his people and give them freedom.

Moses was not at all sure. He had made some really disastrous decisions; and he had a lot of questions about where God had been while his people were in slavery and whether God would really come through for them this time. God did not answer a single one of Moses' questions. He simply told Moses to trust him; and he told him that he had an assignment for him—a plan for his life, to bless him and to use him.

And then Moses asked God a question that God did answer:

"What is your name?"

To which God responded by simply saying, "I AM" (Exodus 3 v 14).

In English we write that as "Jehovah" or (in lots of Bibles) as "LORD." It is a name that God uses to describe himself some 6,519 times in the Old Testament alone. And part of what it means is that God is someone who is all that his people need, and that there is no lack in them that he cannot overcome.

Moses was not convinced that he could do what God was asking. *I am not brave,* he said. *I am not someone who anyone will listen to,* he said. *I am not even any good at public speaking,* he said.

God did not reply with a pep talk. He didn't show Moses his hidden potential. Instead he said, *Moses, I did not choose you because you were any of those things. I am enough of both of those things for the both of us. I AM, and my am-ness overcomes your not-ness.* Ultimately, what matters is who God is, not who Moses is.

I AM... ALL YOU NEED

Throughout Israel's history God would remind them of this name—"I AM," "Jehovah"—whenever Israel was in a time of great distress or fear or need; and whatever they lacked, God would tell them that he would supply it.

He told them he is "Jehovah Mekoddishkem": "I AM the one who changes and purifies you." He could change them when they were stuck.

He told them he is "Jehovah Shammah" (by the end of this chapter, you're going to know more ancient Hebrew words than you had anticipated when you picked this book up): "I AM ever-present." He would be with them when they were alone.

He told them he is "Jehovah Raah": "I AM a shepherd." He would guide them when they felt lost.

He told them he is "Jehovah Jireh": "I AM your provider." He would give them what they needed when they thought there was no way out.

He told them he is "Jehovah Rapha": "I AM your healer." He could help them when they were helpless. He could bind their wounds when they seemed incurable.

He told them he is "Jehovah Shalom" and "Jehovah Sabaoth": "I AM peace" and "I AM your defender." He would give them victory when they faced down their enemies.

For all that Israel needed, for all that they lacked, for all that they could never be in themselves, they had God: the great I AM. The Mighty God.

Just imagine this for a moment: that there really is one God who made and rules everything—and that he is still all these things: a purifying, ever-present, shepherding, providing, healing, defending God.

Wouldn't it be great to have him in your corner?

If he really exists, of course...

Which brings us to Christmas.

OWNING THE STORM

Remember, when Isaiah said, "To us a child is given ... Mighty God," he was saying that one day the great I AM would be born as a tiny baby. The eternal, all-sufficient I AM was going to enter the world as a helpless child.

That is the Bible's claim about the first Christmas. Peer over the manger and you're not just looking at a poor, newborn Jewish boy. You're looking at none other than I AM.

That's the claim. But is it true? There would be an easy way to find out. Could this person do things that only an all-powerful deity could do?

Fast-forward 30 years, and the baby has become a man. He's out on a sea with his friends, the guys we call the "disciples," and there's a terrible storm. Many of the disciples are fishermen by trade, so they know what they're doing on a boat. But this storm is huge, and soon they're all fighting for their lives.

Meanwhile, Jesus is asleep. In all that racket, with the boat pitching and rolling, this is a wonder in itself. Eventually, though, the disciples grow so desperate that they wake him up:

"Teacher! Don't you care that we're going to die?"

Jesus wakes up, looks out at the storm, and says, "Silence! Be still!" The result?

"The wind ceased, and there was a great calm."
(Mark 4 v 38-39)

He looks at the wind and the waves, and he basically says, *Cut it out!* He rebukes the storm.

Rebuke is what you do to somebody whose authority is less than your own. You rebuke your kids: "You will not pee in the sink (again)." You rebuke an employee: "You will not show up late for work." Well, here is a guy who rebukes the weather—and the weather listens to him. He just stands up and turns it off.

It reminds me of standing out in a parking lot when someone's car alarm goes off. Everyone starts grumbling, "Whose car is that?" until someone comes out of a nearby building, looking embarrassed. He mutters something like "Yeah, sorry, that's mine," and presses a button. Bee-beep. Alarm off. That's Jesus' approach here. He stands up and says *It's my storm*—bee-beep. Storm off.

And his disciples, who'd called him a "teacher" in the middle of that storm, now look at each other with a new kind of fear. They ask, "Who then is this? Even the wind and the sea obey him!" (Mark 4 v 41).

They need to follow the evidence of what they've just seen. There's only one being who can stop a storm with a word: the Mighty God. Jehovah. I AM. Jesus is telling them by showing them, *I AM your rescue when you have no hope*. In fact, that's what the name Jesus actually means. The Hebrew version of that name is "Yeshua": "I AM your rescue."

Jesus didn't just claim to be the great I AM, clothed in humanity. He proved that he was who he said he was. Does the great I AM exist? Yes—he came and walked on this earth, and on the pages of history he calmed a storm. He walked on water. He cured blindness and deafness and paralysis. He even raised people from the dead. He did things that we cannot even imagine doing. He is what we are not—the Mighty God.

CHRISTMAS CLARITY, CHRISTMAS HOPE

And so Christmas brings clarity to our questions about God. Is there no God, or many gods? Is there one God— and if so, what is he (or she, or it) actually like? The only way to get beyond guessing is if that God (if he's out there) comes into our existence and reveals himself to us.

In coming to earth as Jesus, that's exactly what he did.

If you find the choice of so many religious options confusing and overwhelming, why not read one of the Gospel accounts of Jesus' life? As you start, say, "Ok, Jesus, can you prove you're the one God, the Mighty God? Show me that I AM is truth, not just a story." Read through his claims and his actions, and think through what you make of them.

The baby born at Christmas doesn't just bring clarity. He also brings hope—because if what Jesus says is true, I AM isn't just about power; it's also about presence. How would life look different if you knew, in every trial, every challenge, every heartache, that he stood by your side? How would it feel to be able to say:

Jesus can heal me of my hurts and scars.

Jesus can change me when I cannot change myself.

Jesus is present with me when I feel all alone.

Jesus is shepherding me when I do not know which way to go.

Jesus is providing for me when I cannot work it out.

Jesus is defending me when I feel defeated.

Jesus is rescuing me from all I need saving from.

For all that I need, for all that I lack, for all that I could never be in myself, Jesus is the great I AM.

One thing that everyone reading this book has in common is this: we each deal with all kinds of insecurities and brokenness. Undoubtedly, you have your own fears and struggles and failings and worries. Maybe you're trying to forget them over the Christmas season. Maybe there are things in your life no one else knows about— things so dark or so painful that you hardly dare admit them to yourself. And you say, "Who on earth is able to help with this? Who could possibly get through that? Who could possibly sort that out? Who is able to find an answer to what I'm facing? I know I am not."

And Jesus says, *I AM*.[4]

"How am I supposed to know which way to go?" *I AM.*

"I'm not really sure who is on my side." *I AM.*

"Nobody's listening to me." *I AM.*

"My marriage is crashing, and I don't know where to turn." *I AM.*

"I'm 50, I'm divorced, and I feel like I'm starting all over." *I AM.*

"Everybody thinks I can't do it." *I AM.*

"What if I fail again?" *I AM.*

"I don't know if I can face the pain in my past." *I AM.*

"I've made so many mistakes." *I AM.*

"I've given all that I could give, and it's not enough." *I AM.*

"I just need a fix or a hit or a drink." *I AM.*

"This Christmas season, I can't hold on." *I AM*. "I'm tired." *I AM*. "I quit." *I AM*. "I feel alone." *I AM*. "I need a fresh start." *I AM*. "I just need somebody to hold me." *I AM*.

Here's what it means to know that Jesus is the Mighty God, who has come to be with us and to prove that he's there and to show us that he cares. It means that for all that you are not, for all that you need, for all that you fear, for all that you crave, he is the great and eternal I AM.

Who else would you rather have on your side?

4. Never (Ever) Disappointing

"Eternal Father"

Here's a word that will produce very, very different reactions from everyone who reads this book: Father.

For some of you, that word makes you smile. You have a great dad, or you are a dad to great kids, or both. When it comes to your own dad, you cherish your memories of him, and you love your time with him. You'd love to spend this Christmas with him.

For some of you, that word makes you smile, but it also makes you sad—because you had a great dad, but he's not around anymore. Your memories of him are beautiful, but you also carry around the memory of his funeral. You'd love to be spending this Christmas with him. But you won't.

And then for some of you, that word brings up a lot of complicated and painful emotions. It makes you want to cry, or to shout, or to shut this book. You did not have a great relationship with your dad, and some of the greatest pain in your life comes from your relationship with him. Maybe he was never there. Maybe he abandoned you when you were very little. Maybe you never even knew him. Maybe you wish you had never known him because he always seemed too busy for you or he was always disappointed in you.

Maybe it was even worse than that. Maybe your father abused his position in your life to abuse you.

If you're in this last category, chances are that the presence—or absence—of your father colors your memories of Christmases past. And so when Isaiah describes Jesus as an "Eternal Father," that just doesn't do much for you.

One of the members of my church wrote a great article about the difficulty that he has had personally in learning to call God "Father" (as Christians tend to—more on that in the next chapter) because of the difficult relationship that he had with his father. Here's what he says:

> "'Father' did not just roll off my tongue the way it did for many of my Christian friends. How could I come to God without fear when I'd been scared to go home whenever Dad was there? How could I understand God's love and faithfulness when Dad left town because he loved something or someone more than me? How can God be a mighty fortress of protection when Dad hit instead of hugged?" [5]

And all that is why the word "Father" provokes such different responses. If it made you smile, then you need to know that the best things about your dad give you a glimpse of what it means for Jesus to be your "Eternal Father." If it made you recoil, then you need to know that Jesus is offering the kind of father-relationship that you need, and have never had.

A few years ago I read a very interesting book called *Father Factor: How Your Father's Legacy Impacts Your Career* by Stephan Poulter. Of course your father's legacy doesn't just impact your career; it impacts your whole life, and it influences your view of God. The famous psychologist Sigmund Freud noted that "Nothing is more common than for a young person to lose faith in God when he loses respect for his father." So, in this chapter, we're going to look at the four types of inadequate fathering that Poulter identifies in that book, and I want to show you each time how Jesus came to offer a very different kind of relationship—and, in that sense, to be a very different kind of father.

THE NEVER-SATISFIED DAD

This is the dad who, no matter what their kids do, never seems to be proud of them. It's never enough for him.

I remember listening to a friend who said that her dad was this way. He was not unkind or abusive. He always provided for her. He never left the family. But, she said,

"I never heard from my dad the words 'I'm proud of you.' That's what I always craved."

She was the first person in her family to go to college and she excelled, exceeding everyone's expectations. As her graduation day approached, she was dreaming about it. Not about walking across the stage or hearing the cheers for the honors she'd gained. She was dreaming about walking off the stage, hoping that she'd see her dad pushing his way through the crowd, rushing up to her, hugging her, and, with tears streaming down his face, saying, "Oh sweetheart, I love you so much, and I am so proud of you!"

When graduation day came, it actually happened like in her dream. She walked down from the stage, and she saw her dad fighting his way through the crowd. But when he reached her, all he said was "It's getting late. Your mom and I have got to go home and try to beat the traffic." That's it. Then he left.

She was absolutely crushed. Years later, she told me, it still affects how she approaches her job, how she relates to her husband, and what she expects from her friends.

For kids who grew up in this kind of home, proving themselves to others often becomes the dominating theme of their lives. Understandably, they carry this perspective of themselves into their relationship with God. Whatever they do, they've got this nagging, unspoken doubt that asks, "Have I done enough for Jesus to accept me? Does Jesus really love me?"

But Jesus could not be more different than the never-satisfied dad. Here is how God treats those who love him:

> "The LORD ... will rejoice over you with gladness.
> He will be quiet in his love.
> He will delight in you with singing."
>
> (Zephaniah 3 v 17)

Do you ache to be special to somebody? To be precious to somebody? You're special, and you're precious to God. Do you yearn to matter? You matter to him. Do you know how much and how often God thinks about you? Before anybody else knew anything about you, he had fashioned you and designed you and laid out every single one of your days. And there's not been a single day of your life when he has not been present. That love is deeper and greater and better than any love anyone has ever received from their earthly father, however great he is.

THE TIME-BOMB DAD

This is the kind of dad from whom you just never knew quite what to expect.

If he had a bad day at work, then the smallest thing would set him off. Maybe drugs or alcohol magnified those outbursts. He hurt his kids verbally, emotionally, or physically. It's hard to love somebody when you're worried that they may, at any moment, begin to attack you. It's still harder to translate this kind of experience into a broader concept of "fatherly love." If your dad explodes all the time, there's nothing safe about the idea of fatherly love.

Stephan Poulter says that the negative ramifications that come from this are manifold. An incredible number of anxiety disorders have their beginnings in this style of fathering. For example, he says, kids who grow up like this often become control freaks. When their dads exploded, their lives crashed, and they were powerless to prevent it. So as soon as they got the chance, they resolved to never be powerless again. They couldn't control dad, but maybe they could control the rest of their lives.

And, of course, experiencing the time-bomb Dad has to affect how you react to the idea of God being a father. You're going to have a hard time trusting him or leaving things in his hands, because how can you trust that he'll actually take care of you? What happens if he's in a bad mood? What happens if he's not consistent? Just like with your earthly dad, you're always trying to figure out what you've got to do to contain him, to stay on his good side, to avoid his outbursts. When you do something wrong, you wonder, *What's coming my way now?* When something in life goes wrong, you wonder, *What did I do now? What's he angry about?*

But Jesus could not be more different than the time-bomb dad. When Moses asked God to show him what he is like, God spoke to him, describing his character. And here's what he told Moses:

> "The LORD is a compassionate and gracious God,
>   slow to anger and abounding in faithful love and
>   truth." (Exodus 34 v 6)

God is quick to love and slow to anger. And he is utterly consistent in who he is and what he's like. "Jesus Christ is the same yesterday, today, and forever" (Hebrews 13 v 8). His reactions are always proportionate to the situation, and he'll respond in the same way tomorrow as he did 2,000 years ago. Jesus abounds constantly in mercy and kindness. Yes, he will get angry, but his anger is not capricious. It doesn't pick on those weaker than him. No, when Jesus gets angry, it's for the sake of justice. It's for the sake of the "little ones" who are being mistreated (Matthew 18 v 6). His anger is never random or out of control.

In fact, the Hebrew word translated as "slow to anger" means "of long nostrils." What do big noses have to do with not being angry?! Think about it: when you get angry, you start breathing heavily, and your nostrils get flared. If you're trying to calm yourself, what are you supposed to do? Take deep breaths: breathe in slowly, in long waves, through your nose. God is of long nostrils—he is calm, and thoughtful, and slow to anger.

None of God's actions towards his people are done in anger. Even when he allows painful things to happen, it is always for the good of those who love him. Every single thing he does for them is done with tenderness and love for their good.

There's assurance in life, and confidence for life, to be found here. God's love is not conditional on anything except you asking him to love you and act toward you as this "father." He doesn't have a temper, he doesn't fly off the handle, and his standards do not change. You can trust him and depend on him.

THE EMOTIONALLY DISTANT DAD

This is the kind of dad who is stable and consistent, who provides for his family, who wouldn't dream of abandoning or abusing his family—but who never says "I love you."

Bo Jackson is still the only man to be an All-Star player in both baseball and American football. Some argue that he is the greatest athlete in history. Maybe so. But that didn't make up for his relationship with his father—or lack of it:

> "My father has never seen me play a football or baseball game. Not a single one. Can you imagine? Here I am, Bo Jackson, one of the so-called premier athletes in the country, and after the game I'm sitting in the locker room and envying every one of my teammates whose dad would come in and talk, have a drink with them after the game. I never experienced that." (Sports Illustrated, 1995)

If our fathers never show affection towards us, we struggle to show affection to others. If we can't open up to our dad, we often don't open up to anyone. When people with this kind of father go through pain, they tend to go through it all alone. They might be extroverts with lots of acquaintances, but they don't really have friends that they go deep with. And, tragically, they often end up being the same type of parent to their own kids.

Jesus isn't like that. Think about what we've already seen of him. He left heaven to live in poverty. Why? So that he could be your Wonderful Counselor. He is the Mighty God who came to earth so that you could know him. What drove him on that journey? Love—love for you.

Jesus once told a story about a father who had a son who wandered off. He left the family home, took his inheritance money, and turned his back on his father. When, a long while later, he decided to return, what happened?

"While the son was still a long way off, his father saw him." (Luke 15 v 20)

It's a little detail, but it tells you so much about this father; he had stood at the gate of his home every day, just looking into the distance, longing for his son to appear on the horizon. He couldn't get on with his life and he couldn't move from his vantage point, because he was so emotionally connected to his child. He could not rest until his son had been restored.

And then, when he saw his son appear one day, the father "was filled with compassion. He ran, threw his arms around his neck, and kissed him." He lifted up the edges of his robes, and he sprinted to his son. In those days, men of position and prestige did not run. This father didn't care. He happily embraced ridicule and shame in order to bring his son back home. That's how connected he was to his son.

As Jesus tells this story, his message is *I am like that father.*

Here is something amazing: the Mighty God is so emotionally connected to you that he has bound up his emotions in yours, so that he will not rest until you have been brought home, back into the family. That's how much he loves you. That's how much he wants to spend his time with you. In fact, he's done everything necessary to spend the whole of eternity with you.

THE ABSENT DAD

This is the dad who just wasn't there.

Nearly 40% of children in the United States live in fatherless homes. In these situations, kids often subconsciously interpret the absence of their dad as a personal rejection. They think they weren't important enough for Dad to stay. They weren't good enough. They may never articulate it, and most likely nobody ever says that to them, but that's what they end up thinking.

Counselors say this often manifests itself as a sort of background sadness. The counseling pastor at the church I serve, Brad Hambrick, says it's like a soundtrack that plays in the back of the heart. When you're watching a movie scene, the soundtrack tells you—at a visceral level—how you're supposed to interpret it. It doesn't matter if I'm watching a happy couple walk through the park; layer the Jaws theme onto that and I'm expecting something terrible. Change the soundtrack and you change the mood.

For those whose dads simply weren't there, there is often a soundtrack of sadness lying under every episode in life. So it doesn't matter if things are going well or not. At a deep, inarticulate level, there's a sense that it's all just on the cusp of going wrong.

An absent dad can leave us feeling angry, or anxious, or incredibly driven to be better, to do better, to prove ourselves. As Will Smith put it in one of the most famous episodes of *The Fresh Prince of Bel-Air*, when his father has just walked out on him for the second time in his life:

> *"Who needs him? He wasn't there to teach me how to shoot my first basket, but I learned. I got through my first date without him. I learned how to drive, learned how to shave, learned how to fight without him. I had 14 great birthdays*

without him ... I didn't need him then, and I don't need him now ... I'm going to get through college without him. I'm going to get a great job without him. I'm going to marry me a beautiful honey and have a whole bunch of kids, and I don't need him for any of that... How come he don't want me?"

Now listen to Jesus. He showed up, and he stayed. He only left his friends once, because he was hung up on a cross. And even then, he made sure they knew why he was leaving. Speaking of eternal life beyond death, he said:

"I am going away to prepare a place for you. If I go away and prepare a place for you, I will come again and take you to myself, so that where I am you may be also." (John 14 v 2-3)

Not only that, but he assured them that, beyond his death, he would come and live with them again, not physically but spiritually, through his Spirit. "I will not leave you as orphans," he promised them: "I am coming to you" (14 v 18). Or, as Hebrews 13 v 5 puts it, "I will never leave you or abandon you."

That's the father that we all crave. That's the relationship that Jesus was born to beckon you into. That is the one that you've always been searching for.

And once you've discovered it, it lasts forever. This is what unites those of you with terrible dads with those of you who have fantastic dads—because even the best dads die. They won't be around forever—and the better the father, the bigger the hole they leave behind them. Maybe this Christmas, as you look round the table and he's not there, you know all too painfully the truth of that. And so the word "eternal" is precious to all of us. Jesus doesn't leave, disappoint, fail, hurt—or die. He's eternal.

CHRISTMAS IN A FOREIGN COUNTRY

A few years back some friends of ours, Ryan and Morgan, adopted a child from an orphanage in another country. They'd passed through all the legal processes in that country. Charlie was their son.

But right before the day when they were supposed to pick Charlie up from the orphanage, things changed. There were some political upheavals, and the country froze the process. No more children were going to be able to leave the country.

Charlie could not come to Ryan and Morgan. So they decided to go to him. They flew over from the US and basically camped out outside of the orphanage, spending half their time with their son and the other half lobbying the courts and meeting with government officials, pleading with them to release their son.

After a few weeks Morgan came home, but Ryan stayed. It was at Christmas time. This was not where he wanted to be at Christmas—away from home, far from family. But here was a father who loved his son, and since his son could not come to him, he was going to go to that son, and he was going to fight for that son.

There would be more days and weeks of struggle, but, wonderfully, Ryan was eventually able to bring Charlie home.

That Christmas, as Ryan battled corrupt court systems on the other side of the world, it struck me that he was a picture of the kind of "Eternal Father" that Jesus is for anyone who asks him to be. Jesus went far further for us than Ryan went for his son. He didn't leave a country of privilege to move to a country of poverty—no, he left the riches of heaven to come to a world of pain. He did all that because he loves us. He did all that because he wants to be with us. He came to us to ensure that we could go to be with him, and it cost him far more than a plane ticket, as we'll see in the next chapter.

Jesus is the Eternal Father. The best earthly father is just a faint echo of the way he loves us. The most disappointing earthly father can be a reminder that there is someone who has never disappointed, and never will. He offers to love you like a perfect father, forever.

5. Accepted and Welcomed

"Prince of Peace"

Bart Ehrman is a bestselling author in the United States who has made his fortune questioning what the Gospels tell us about Jesus. Because he and I both live in the Raleigh-Durham area in North Carolina, I have had the chance to attend many of his events. Once he was asked, "What would it take to get you to believe in Jesus?"

His answer was simple, and really revealing:

> *"If Jesus had fulfilled his promise to bring peace on earth."*

Here's the problem that many have with Jesus: he was supposed to be the "Prince of Peace," but he didn't seem to deliver. When he was born, the angelic choir famously pronounced that he had brought "peace on earth" (Luke 2 v 14). And yet, 2,000 years later, the guns still do not fall silent, not even on Christmas Day. Relational strife and domestic violence still impact more households than most of us realize. Poverty still afflicts millions of people throughout the world. Injustice is still the daily experience of huge swathes of our societies.

So why didn't Jesus fulfill the promise of the title that Isaiah gave him: the Prince of Peace? Was bringing peace on earth just too big a task?

Actually, when we think of peace that way, we are looking at something much smaller than what Isaiah had in mind.

YOUR BIGGEST PROBLEM MIGHT BE DIFFERENT THAN YOU THOUGHT

Here's a secret I've learned in my life. I've seen it played out hundreds of times in the church that I pastor. Horizontal dysfunction very often goes back to a vertical disconnect from God. In other words, we don't see the peace of God in our lives and in our world (the horizontal aspect of our lives) because we do not enjoy peace with God (the vertical aspect).

Our greatest relational problem is our lack of relationship with God. Our greatest poverty is the spiritual poverty of not knowing God. The greatest injustice is the way that we—I, and you—have treated the One who made us, who made this world, and who loves us so much that he came to live with us.

Here's my question for you. What if all the problems in your life ultimately stemmed from, or at least were exacerbated by, the reality that you are separated from God?

Some of the most insightful or influential secular writers of our time have pointed out that a lot of our drive in life, and a lot of our angst and dysfunction, goes back to a fear that we are not accepted. The famous playwright Arthur Miller (who wrote *Death of a Salesman*) stopped believing in God as a teenager. But, decades later, he said this:

> "I feel like I've carried around this sense of judgment. I could not escape it. I still felt like I needed to prove myself to others: to have somebody tell me that I was okay, that I was acceptable, that I was approved of."

He had replaced the God of Christmas with the "god" of audience approval. He was still looking for someone to tell him that he was accepted, and not under judgment. He never quite found it.

Madonna said this in *Vanity Fair* magazine:

> "All of my will has always been to conquer some horrible feeling of inadequacy. I'm always struggling with that fear ... My drive in life is from this horrible fear of being mediocre. And that's always pushing me, pushing me. Because even though I've become Somebody, I still have to prove that I'm Somebody. My struggle has never ended and it probably never will."[6]

We're all looking for acceptance. Deep down, I want to suggest that we're all looking for the most important acceptance there is—acceptance from the One who made us, who knows us, and who rules eternity. We want peace—we need peace—with God.

This is actually a bigger problem than most of us realize. The truth is, each of us has pursued a life of conflict with God. We don't want him to be in charge. We don't want to need him. We don't want him to get to state the rules. We don't want him to get the praise. No—we want to be in charge, we want to be independent, we want to decide what's right and wrong, and we want to enjoy the praise.

That attitude is what the Bible calls "sin." It is the universal human condition of all people, whether or not they consider themselves religious. (If you don't believe me, try living in the way that God lays out in the Bible for 24 hours—not just in what you do, but in what you say and think, too. I couldn't do it, and you'll find you cannot either.)

The irony is that we turn away from God to get more freedom, approval, and acceptance. But we find the opposite. Shutting God out, we feel vulnerable. Exposed. Ashamed. Under judgment. In darkness. Always seeking more and never truly finding it. Our struggle, like Madonna's, never ends, and it never will.

We were made to enjoy the love and acceptance of God—to live at peace with God. But we have mistreated him even as we live in his world—so what would it take to return to that peace?

Forgiveness.

And that is why Jesus came. This is what his title of "Prince of Peace" points us to. Into the darkness of a world in rebellion against God, God sent a child. He would live the most unusual life. He would not be born into power and privilege the way you would expect the son of a deity to be born. He would not rule from a throne. He would be born in poverty. He would make his life with the guilty and the oppressed. And he would eventually die, unjustly, a criminal's death, even though nobody was able to point out anything he had ever said or done wrong.

It sounds like a tragic end, but it was not—it was a God-ordained end. The Old Testament is full of pictures of what God's Son would achieve, and Isaiah provides us with one of the most evocative:

> "He was pierced because of our rebellion,
>   crushed because of our iniquities;
>   punishment for our peace was on him,
>   and we are healed by his wounds." (Isaiah 53 v 5)

This is the purpose for which Jesus was born and for which he died: to take the punishment necessary to bring us peace with God. Christmas was always going to lead to Easter. So to understand the core of Christmas, you'll need to look at Easter.

FORGIVENESS ALWAYS COMES AT A COST

But, as I remember a Muslim asking me when I lived in Southeast Asia, why would God need somebody to die in order to forgive our sin?

He put it this way: "If you sinned against me, and I wanted to forgive you, I wouldn't make you kill your dog before I forgave you. Why would God require some kind of sacrifice to forgive?"

Here's how I answered him.

Choosing to forgive somebody means that you are agreeing to absorb the cost of the injustice of what they've done. Imagine you stole my car and you wrecked it, and you don't have insurance and or the money to pay for it. What are my choices?

I could make you pay. I could haul you before a judge and request a court-mandated payment plan. If you were foolish enough to steal my $1.5 million Ferrari (No, I do not actually own a Ferrari), you might never pay it off, and you'd always be in my debt.

But I have another choice.

I could forgive you. (I might not—please don't steal my family's Honda Odyssey to find out.) What am I choosing to do if I say, "I forgive you"? I'm not just sending good feelings your way. I'm choosing to absorb the cost of your wrong. If I don't hold you accountable for paying for the damage, I'll have to pay the price of having the car fixed. I'll take the hit for the injustice you did me. You have no debt to pay—not because there was nothing to pay, but because I paid it all. Not only that, I'm choosing to absorb the pain of your treatment of me. I have the right to say, "We cannot be friends now. You won't be coming into my house anymore." But instead, I'm choosing to give you friendship and acceptance even though you deserve the opposite.

This is always how forgiveness works. It comes at a cost. If you forgive someone, you bear the cost rather than insisting that the wrongdoer does.

And that is what Jesus, the Mighty God, was doing when he came to earth and lived as a man and died a criminal's death on a wooden cross.

I WILL TAKE IT

On the cross, the Mighty God absorbed the pain and the penalty for our rebellion against his rule and our rejection of his love. God said, *It will go no farther than here. You deserve punishment, but I will take it. You deserve separation, but I will take it. You do not deserve welcome or acceptance, but I will offer it.*

That's why Jesus cried out as he died, "My God, My God, why have you abandoned me?" (Matthew 27 v 46). He was going through hell, because hell is total separation from God's love and acceptance. It's where we're headed because we have chosen to walk away from God. It's what God himself went through in our place. God was separated from God.

How does that work?! Here's how: God is one God in three "Persons"—the Father, the Son (who we usually call "Jesus"), and the Spirit. We often call this truth about who God is the "Trinity," and it's not possible to adequately describe this in a couple of hundred words—in fact, it's not possible to fully understand without our human minds imploding. But what we can understand is that this means that God is a God of relationship, who has been enjoying a perfectly loving relationship as Father, Son, and Spirit since— well, since forever. For all time (and since before time), the Father has been loving the Son and the Spirit, and they have been loving him back.

Until, on the cross, "the punishment that brought us peace was upon him." This is what it cost Jesus, God the Son, to bring us home. This is what it cost Jesus so that God—Father, Son, and Spirit—to relate to us as the "eternal father" we've always longed for.

As Jesus hung on the cross that Friday afternoon, about 30 years after he had lain in a wooden manger, the debt of sin was paid. Some of Jesus' last words before he died were "It is finished" (John 19 v 30). Actually, what he would have said in Greek is just one word: *Tetelestai*. It was the word that was scribbled on a tax bill when it was paid. It meant the debt was cleared—all gone. So Jesus was looking at your sin and he was saying: *It is paid. The debt is cleared. You can be forgiven.*

This is what makes Christianity unique. Jesus' message

is the opposite of what every other religious leader has taught. For instance, take the Buddha's final words: "Strive without ceasing." But Jesus said, *I have done the striving for you, and now it is finished. I have done it for you.*

So when God promised through Isaiah that a child would be born who would be called the Prince of Peace, he was not talking about that child's earthly rise to power. He was talking about that child's sacrificial death on our behalf.

Christmas doesn't make sense without Easter. Jesus being the Prince of Peace doesn't make sense until we realize that the peace he came to bring was the peace we most need, a solution to humanity's deepest problem—not a vaccine for a virus, but forgiveness for our sin. He came to offer the peace that meets our greatest needs and that will last for eternity—peace with God.

PEACE NOW, PEACE TO COME

When we are at peace with God, everything changes.

We know we are accepted in the eyes of the only person whose opinion ultimately really matters.

We know that whatever we pass through in life and however we come to death, a welcome awaits us in eternity.

We know that we need not fear eternal darkness anymore.

We know we are a somebody, because we know that Jesus loves us enough to die for us.

You may have noticed this if you know someone who has started to follow Jesus: when somebody finds peace with God, they start displaying the peace of God. The vertical transforms the horizontal. They become more loving husbands. They become more content wives. They become gentler parents; they become more forgiving. That's because our souls were made for God and—as the fourth-century African bishop, Augustine, put it—our hearts are restless until we find our rest in him.

One day, the peace we all yearn for will finally come. Peace on earth will come, and it will be final. The baby who grew to die on the cross also rose from a grave[7], and he will one day come again to his world, not in weakness as a baby but in power as a king. On that day, this child will restore the earth to the way it was intended to be. He will right all wrongs; he will end all diseases; he will restore justice. Peace on earth will be a reality. But before he came to institute the peace of God on earth, he came to die for our sin to bring us peace with God, so that we can enjoy that life with God on earth when he returns.

What if all of the problems in your life ultimately stemmed from, or at least were exacerbated by, the reality that you are separated from God?

And what if the Prince of Peace died to offer you an acceptance from God, and a peace with God, that will change your life now and then stretch on into perfection, forever?

6. What Do You Call God?

I can tell a lot about someone's relationship with me simply by what they call me.

I don't usually answer phone calls from numbers I don't recognize. But every now and then, when I feel like tempting fate, I'll pick up. Often, I hear a voice on the other end ask if this is "Mr Gree-ar."

Two syllables—Gree... Ar.

Immediately, I know that the person on the other end is a telemarketer who doesn't know me at all. I know that because although my surname has a strange number of consecutive vowels in it, it's pronounced as one syllable. The guy on the other end of the phone had to pick a way to pronounce a surname with three vowels in a row in it—and he picked wrong. He may be a very bright guy, but he clearly does not know me.

Occasionally somebody will call me "Dr. Greear." At that point I know they've done a little homework on me—they know my educational qualifications. (It's a Ph.D., by the way—I'm not a medical doctor, so please don't send me pictures of a strange rash.) But I also know they don't know me that well, because literally nobody in my life refers to me as Dr. Greear.

And every now and then, I get a message or an email, and it begins like this:

"J. Dizzle..."

When I hear or see that, I know that it's a message from an old friend, because when I was younger I had a group of friends who called me J. Dizzle. Call me that and I know that you know me well—that we're close. (Or I know that you read this book and you reached this final chapter. In which case, I count you as a friend, too.)

There are four people in the world who call me "Daddy." Those people are the most precious little people in the world to me. They know me in a unique way: better and closer than almost anyone else ever could. (And, of course, there is the inner circle of inner circles—the one and only person in the world allowed to call me "The Silver Fox"—my wife, Veronica. On this earth, no one knows me better or loves me more.)

Names matter. What you call someone matters. What you call them reveals the nature of your relationship with them.

So here's my question, as we reach the end of our time together: *What do you call God?*

There are four Gospels in the New Testament, and only two of them (Matthew and Luke) tell us the Christmas story. Of the other two, Mark skips

Christmas altogether and gets straight to the adult Jesus calling people to follow him. And John majors on the significance and the implications of the first Christmas rather than the events themselves:

"He [God] was in the world, and the world was created through him," he tells us. But in his day, as in ours, people did not want him around: "The world did not recognize him." Even the religious Jews, the descendants of Moses and Isaiah, were not interested in rearranging their lives to live under his rule: "He came to his own, and his own people did not receive him" (John 1 v 10-11).

But that wasn't the end of the story:

> "To all who did receive him, he gave them the right
> to be children of God, to those who believe in his
> name." (v 12)

Believing in his name does not just mean that you believe he existed. Or that he was special. Or that he can help you. Or even that he rose from the dead. It means that you "receive him" into your life: you recognize that he is the Wonderful Counselor, the Mighty God, the Eternal Father, the Prince of Peace, and you ask him to be those things for you. It means that you realize that, whatever you've been searching for in life, you will find it in knowing the One who is at the center of the first Christmas—that in a sense, all along you've been searching for Christmas.

Jesus is who he is. That's not up for a vote. But he

won't be those things *for you* until you receive him—until you believe in him.

So the question I'm asking is not simply if you believe all of those things to be true about Jesus. I'm asking you if you have received those things for yourself.

Is he your Wonderful Counselor, to whom you give the right to guide and direct your life?

Is he your Mighty God, whom you trust to be all that you need, because you know that you're not enough on your own?

Is he your Eternal Father, the one whose love will awaken, encourage, and sustain you?

Is he your Prince of Peace, whom you are asking to die in your place so you can be forgiven and accepted eternally?

Because if he is, you can look at the great I AM, the God who made you and everything around you, and who rules today and every day on into eternity, and you can call him... Daddy.

Of course, not everyone receives Jesus. In fact, most don't—including, surprisingly, many religious people, good people, clever people. "He came to his own, and his own people did not receive him." But maybe you know that *you* need to receive him as your Wonderful Counselor, Mighty God, Eternal Father, and Prince of peace. If that's you, you can say something to him like the prayer below. These are not magic words. But if they come from your heart, he'll hear them.

Lord Jesus, I know that I'm a sinner, and I know that I need you. I accept you as my Wonderful Counselor—come and guide my life. I know you are the Mighty God—you have the right to rule me. I need you as my Eternal Father—thank you for loving me. I ask you to be my Prince of Peace—please forgive me. Amen.

> *"A child will be born for us,*
> *a son will be given to us …*
> *He will be named*
> *Wonderful Counselor, Mighty God,*
> *Eternal Father, Prince of Peace."*

Endnotes

1 Craig Groeschel, "Wonderful Counselor," from the "He Will Be Called" sermon series, preached at Life Church.

2 Here are the Bible verses that I quote in each of the claims I make about Jesus on page 22: John 14 v 6; Isaiah 53 v 3,4 (ESV translation); Matthew 11 v 28; Hebrews 7 v 25 (ESV).

3 Food processors: amazon.com/s?k=food+processor&i=garden&crid=24K617SWR9FDX&sprefix=food+processor%2Caps%2C165&ref=nb_sb_ss_c_2_14
Drills: amazon.com/s?k=drill&i=tools&ref=nb_sb_noss_1
(Both accessed May 12, 2020.)

4 I am indebted in the following list to Louie Giglio, who made the timeless truth of God's "I AM" come alive in his book I Am Not But I Know I Am (Multnomah, 2012).

5 thegospelcoalition.org/article/is-god-the-father-like-my-father/ (accessed May 12, 2020).

6 https://archive.vanityfair.com/article/share/bd86a835-b84c-47a7-bbec-60b9af6ea282 (accessed March 9, 2020).

7 If you want to read more about the resurrection, I'd recommend N.T. Wright's stellar book, The Resurrection of the Son of God (Fortress Press, 2003). For a more accessible book on the topic, check out Lee Strobel's The Case for Christ (Zondervan, 1998).

the**good**book
COMPANY

Thanks for reading this book. We hope you enjoyed it, and found it helpful.

Most people want to find answers to the big questions of life: Who are we? Why are we here? How should we live? But for many valid reasons we are often unable to find the time or the right space to think positively and carefully about them.

Perhaps you have questions that you need an answer for. Perhaps you have met Christians who have seemed unsympathetic or incomprehensible. Or maybe you are someone who has grown up believing, but need help to make things a little clearer.

At The Good Book Company, we're passionate about producing materials that help people of all ages and stages understand the heart of the Christian message, which is found in the pages of the Bible.

Whoever you are, and wherever you are at when it comes to these big questions, we hope we can help. As a publisher we want to help you look at the good book that is the Bible because we're convinced that as we meet the person who stands at its heart—Jesus Christ—we find the clearest answers to our biggest questions.

Visit our website to discover the range of books, videos and other resources we produce, or visit our partner site www.christianityexplored.org for a clear explanation of who Jesus is and why he came.

Thanks again for reading,

Your friends at The Good Book Company

thegoodbook.com | thegoodbook.co.uk
thegoodbook.com.au | thegoodbook.co.nz | thegoodbook.co.in

WWW.CHRISTIANITYEXPLORED.ORG

Our partner site is a great place to explore the Christian faith, with powerful testimonies and answers to difficult questions.